CW01263242

TEACHERS WHO CHANGED LIVES

TEACHERS WHO CHANGED LIVES

Stories of Inspirational Educators

AVERY NIGHTINGALE

Creative Quill Press

CONTENTS

1	Introduction	1
2	Early Years	2
3	The Power of Encouragement	4
4	Fostering Creativity	5
5	Embracing Diversity	7
6	Instilling a Love for Learning	9
7	Nurturing Confidence	10
8	Overcoming Challenges	12
9	Making Learning Fun	13
10	Creating a Supportive Environment	14
11	Empowering Students	15
12	Teaching Life Skills	16
13	Inspiring Future Generations	18
14	Cultivating Critical Thinking	20
15	Promoting Collaboration	22
16	Adapting to Individual Needs	23
17	Building Resilience	24

18	Encouraging Self-Reflection	25
19	Fostering a Growth Mindset	27
20	Teaching Beyond the Classroom	29
21	Emphasizing Character Development	31
22	Encouraging Curiosity	33
23	Supporting Student Goals	35
24	Igniting Passion for a Subject	36
25	Creating a Sense of Belonging	38
26	Teaching Empathy and Compassion	39
27	Promoting Global Awareness	41
28	Building Positive Relationships	42
29	Celebrating Achievements	44
30	Leaving a Lasting Impact	46
31	Conclusion	47

Copyright © 2024 by Avery Nightingale

All rights reserved. No part of this book may be reproduced in any manner whatsoever without written permission except in the case of brief quotations embodied in critical articles and reviews.

First Printing, 2024

CHAPTER 1

Introduction

This introduction expresses what it means to be a teacher and suggests that most members of the profession rarely understand the profound impact that they have had on students' lives. The introduction also hints at a wide definition of "inspiration" in its examination of how these teachers have affected others. The introduction describes the concept of changing the world by affecting an individual, a view that is returned to at the end of the book in the final chapter entitled "Changing the World." Though the introduction sets the stage for the rest of the book, detailing the types of teachers and students who will be examined and explaining the book's organization, the introduction is the only stage at which the book's organization is not described in relation to the lives of specific teachers that will be analyzed.

CHAPTER 2

Early Years

The same holds true for Benjamin O. Canada who grew up in segregated Virginia. He recalls with admiration his 7th grade shop teacher who he believes was determined not to let his students become products of their environment, emphasizing education as the way to advance in life. This special teacher took students to the "white only school" to prepare them for the future in the integrated school system and credited with getting each and every student to college. According to Canada, this man's message was clear, "We are preparing to compete blockade as it called for us to integrate under the public school policy and we have to be ready."

Each of the teachers profiled remember at least one influential educator from their formative years "who first stimulated my curiosity and made me want to learn more." Dr. Kay Toliver recalls how a "well organized" teacher in 6th grade was the first to teach her fractions. This teacher had a plan. He took me step by step and taught me everything I needed to know so that it just made sense and I've never had any problems with fractions since. That was math class at its best."

To no one's surprise, the common denominator for all teachers profiled in the book is intelligence. Raised by parents who either strongly encouraged education or were educators themselves, it appears that teaching was the only profession with which they would find fulfillment.

Childhood

CHAPTER 3

The Power of Encouragement

But Mr. Buchanan did not call the boy to his chair. Instead, the headmaster drew up an old wicker armchair, offered the boy his cheroot and one of his books, and thus did their daily concerts begin. It could not be said in truth that the boy was one of Mr. Buchanan's affectionate or even properly poor. He was the son of a well-known Scottish architect, and Mr. Buchanan would be the last man to sacrifice good relations with an influential parishioner for the pleasure of being the friend of his offspring. But Mr. Buchanan had the heart of a lover of youth. And he had seen the boy's glance at the music-master's window.

The young teen knew he was caught. He had been playing his guitar in the girls' toilets, and though the other kids had acclaimed his impromptu concert, Mr. Buchanan, the headmaster, was not amused. Plunged into inner misery, the boy loitered under the trees at lunchtime, knowing that Mr. Buchanan would pass his well-known spot as he took his daily constitution on the playing fields, and then the head would summon him to his chair of judgment.

CHAPTER 4

Fostering Creativity

Teacher influence, on its most basic level, is getting the student to understand the material in the best way. The best way will be different for all students and for all material. At times, the best way for a student to understand a concept will be to use a method unconventional to the standard or at the least, the most effective way will involve the student creating his or her own actions, method or ideas to demonstrate the concept of understanding. Successful students will also use creativity in their professional lives to solve problems or to communicate complex ideas in a simple manner. Thus, creative thought and action are the goals of learning. Creativity in any field is a result of discipline, effort and mastery of fundamentals. A progressive educator recognizes that a student's seemingly wasteful digressions may be the first step in the development of a new and more effective way to do something. It has been said that if you ask a silly question, you get a silly answer. This is not always a bad thing. A silly question, while not direct, could lead to a more exciting and engaging investigation of the topic. At which point, the student will have sparked into a more enlightened mode of thinking and zero creativity is fully disengaged. This is a rare thing to happen in a traditional classroom so teachers must be aware of this happening and promote an open environment where student errors are seen as positive progressions towards true understanding.

It is difficult to imagine a quality of genuine greatness which would not include originality - John W. Gardner.

CHAPTER 5

Embracing Diversity

The idea of cultural discontinuity is influenced and mediated by a number of factors, including the school's expectations and the potential socioeconomic impact. Each case of cultural discontinuity can have different effects on a child, from a lack of motivation and low self-esteem to externalizing and internalizing behavior. The negative effects can have lasting damage and seriously hinder learning and educational progress. An understanding of cultural discontinuity on the part of teachers, through greater insight into the cultural background of the child, can prevent such cases and foster conditions more conducive to learning. This chapter is then translated into real life through the sharing of personal accounts of school and student experiences in a similar context to cultural discontinuity. Through its provision of practical examples, the current and prospective educator can learn how to better understand their students and thus create a more effective teaching environment. This chapter is highly valuable to any teacher working in multicultural settings and can provide insight for those in more monocultural environments to better assist those of differing backgrounds.

Embracing diversity introduces the concept that knowledge of the students' cultural background is vital and that sound teaching must acknowledge and build upon the pupils' own ways of learning. This can have a very powerful and positive effect on the education process of children from all cultures and socioeconomic groups. The value placed upon formal education, the role of parents, and self-expectation are just some of the underlying factors that contribute to the ways in which children become effective learners. This is explored in the first chapter, which introduces the idea of cultural discontinuity; an experience common in children of minority cultural backgrounds.

CHAPTER 6

Instilling a Love for Learning

In this final section, Harmin returns to the themes of dedication and caring which imbue all the stories. The educators portrayed all took a personal interest in the needs, hopes, and problems of their students. They sought to help them achieve what they really wanted to achieve and, at times, what they ought to achieve. This required an attitude of caring conviction for the student and the long and hard task of discovering what the student's goals really were. "Teachers who Changed Lives" is a book that is not only a testament to the remarkable work of the teachers it portrays but a source of inspiration for practicing teachers at all levels and in a variety of disciplines today. Poring over the pages, the reader is struck with the realization that teaching is indeed a noble and wondrous calling. At a time when society often seems to have given up on the ideal of an educated populace and fallen into a resigned acceptance of widespread ignorance and poor academic achievement, this is a book that serves as a clarion call to the belief that given the right conditions and the right person to inspire, it is indeed possible for people to learn and learn well.

CHAPTER 7

Nurturing Confidence

An Introduction to Nurturing Confidence "Nurturing confidence is an essential aspect of teaching. Teachers who instill a sense of belief and conviction in their students encourage them to fulfill their potential. Confidence sustains and nurtures self-belief and a sense of personal self-worth. This is particularly important as it affects the energy and direction students put into their learning as well as their levels of aspiration and achievement. Consequently, raising students' confidence increases their capacity to learn with many related benefits in terms of motivation and results. Mr. Ted Fullerton, an English teacher and a Deputy Head in Dunedin, New Zealand from 1959 to 1986, developed close relationships with his students, encouraging them to develop personal sets of values. Fullerton sought to teach students "not just to know but also to appraise and have conviction about what they believe in." Mr. Fullerton believed in every student and sought to acknowledge their individuality. He also placed high importance on the ability to explain and defend their point of view. He was tremendously successful in instilling belief and self-sufficiency in students that has persisted throughout their lives. Mr. Fullerton maintained an aura of "cool" and always found time to talk with students outside of the classroom. He was always able to relate to and converse with anyone, a feature he hoped to instill in his students. Fullerton's underlying sense of expectation and the pride he had in his students were perhaps the greatest catalysts for the confidence that they developed."

CHAPTER 8

Overcoming Challenges

"The kids were so much more interested in tearing each other down and backbiting than in their academics - they considered them all too stupid to be worth their serious time," she said. "I remember asking them questions about what good education and a good life were for them, and the prospects of it for twenty minutes when a class clown threw a paper airplane across the room and I lost it. I berated them for ten minutes about how they could tolerate their communication and behavior, but at the end of the day they were still only ninth graders and I was taking my struggles with them too seriously. At that point, I just felt sick and hypocritical; who was I to tell them what was good for them and what they needed when I was so disillusioned and angry at the time?".

When Virginia Marie "Ginny" Leighton was in the Distinguished Teacher Program at Elmhurst College in Elmhurst, Illinois, she decided to drop out. There was not a dramatic moment - she was not a troubled student or an unhappy person at the time - but she just made a decision that made sense. Her plan was to go to graduate school to be a therapist rather than a teacher. She reasoned that she had always been good at advising and helping others in their personal lives, but she had also reached her boiling point after one experience in a ninth-grade class at York Community High School.

CHAPTER 9

Making Learning Fun

Another way to teach a subject creatively is to incorporate the subject in a fun activity. One might be surprised at how well this can actually be done if one really tries to apply it.

Mr. Baraboo went to great lengths to make his class loads of fun, not only by teaching life lessons through his own personal experiences, but also by teaching the curriculum in a way that was easy to understand and fun to learn. For example, when teaching a unit on World War II, Mr. Baraboo had the students dress up as Nazis and Storm Troopers and had them all videotape a mock interview with Adolf Hitler explaining the rise and fall of the Nazi party. Although this can be viewed as controversial, it is a creative enough assignment where the students are going to want to truly learn the material to make the assignment believable and get a better understanding of it.

One of the best ways to make a subject fun is to teach it differently. Often times, new teachers or teachers that are new to teaching a subject will simply use the curriculum or textbook as a reference for plans. A teacher who likes to have fun with their subject and truly make it a great learning experience needs to think outside the box and create assignments that will make the students want to learn more.

CHAPTER 10

Creating a Supportive Environment

My grade 11 law teacher, Mr. Wark, gave students multiple ways to contact him. Because he had such a busy schedule, he was rarely available during lunch hours. Although he still encouraged students to drop by during that time, he even put a mini fridge stocked with their favorite soft drinks in his classroom, with a note "if I'm not here, grab a soda and check my office". Somehow, even when he wasn't there, students still found soda money in their pockets. Mr. Wark would give students his home phone number, which soon became a problem as students from current and previous years would call him up to the late hours of the night and during dinner with law questions. He didn't have the heart to turn off his home phone to students, so eventually he had to give it up to telemarketers and get a new number. Although this story may seem extreme and dangerous, the ability to contact him proved to come in handy when students needed law questions answered by test time and no help available.

CHAPTER 11

Empowering Students

Empowering students to uncover their capacity for success is another theme that emerges. These educators are facilitators who do not find their own gratification in control or compliance, rather in efforts to grant students the power to solve their own problems and to find self-directing ways and means to learn new information or material. They encourage students through emphasizing the dynamic nature of real learning and by demonstrating open-mindedness and respect for students' views and statements. Such teachers understand that empowering students to master new information or to develop new capabilities requires that they attend to and work on the students' beliefs in their own efficacy to carry out learning tasks. This often involves showing students - through direct instruction and graduated content mastery, and by providing constructive feedback on performance - how to break learning into smaller more manageable tasks and how to self-monitor their competence in carrying them out. An emphasis on empowering students to learn is a long-term proposition; its efficacy can often best be judged by the extent to which former students become self-regulating learners in the years following their formal education.

CHAPTER 12

Teaching Life Skills

Teaching life skills is an important aspect of education. In his interview, Dr. Elliot Washor tells a story from his earlier years of teaching of a young man who, after spending many months in a traditional English classroom, was still unable to begin his essay with a topic sentence. This student's primary form of communication was through his hands, as he was a carpenter. Dr. Washor suggested that this student would write a "how to" essay on a favorite project of his. After spending many years teaching students traditional English essays, Dr. Washor says he has realized that this student and other students in vocational-technical programs would be better off learning to write the sort of essay that he asked this student to write, as it would be more directly related to the writing they would be required to do on the job. The life skill in question here is writing. By convincing the student to use writing as a tool to create a "how to" guide, his level of engagement in writing was raised to the highest levels. Writing was no longer something he "had" to do to pass a class. He was now using writing as a means to accomplish an end, and after writing instructions for his entire project, he noticed that he had significantly improved his English, an unintended consequence. This student may not have learned this form of writing in a standard English class with a rubric and a teacher-designed thesis; it was only when he decided to complete his project more efficiently. This writing would not have been done if it were not for the conversation between the student and the teacher. This conversation was a form of Socratic Dialogue/coaching, with the primary goal to improve the quality of the student's thinking and the level of engagement in his work.

CHAPTER 13

Inspiring Future Generations

Howard Wilson's essay, "What Does Your Education Mean To You," revealed a theme in which he discusses that education does not mold our lives but instead it shapes the personalities of who we are. Continuing with the same ideology, Pillow's article "Cultivating Humanity" supports the same views as Wilson's, as she emphasizes that education should focus on teaching students, which should help them become more human and enhance personal growth, self-worth, and improvement. Both authors take consideration of the role of the teacher in the student's life and how higher education that focuses on more personal growth is a tool to enhance the students' learning capability that would not have been possible without those environments. According to Pillow, what makes a teacher a good educator is someone who is caring and compassionate and considers the understanding of their students to the best of their abilities, stating that it's the "knowledge of that world that draws students into genuine conversation and critical reflection." She calls these academicians the "moral sponsors" of their students, who animate their moral, intellectual, and social growth, someone who cultivates humanity. Pillow's ideas are consistent with those of Wilson's, where he describes an educator that transformed his life. He stated the professor was not just a teacher but a mentor and friend who transformed his outlook on life and helped shape his character. Both authors agree that the growth of a student should be a positive transformation.

CHAPTER 14

Cultivating Critical Thinking

In an article about the importance of teaching critical thinking through decision-making in mini-debates, Ian James and Jim Duggan describe competing ideas or opinions as a useful learning tool and resource to prompt thoughtful judgment and choice between alternatives. In this exercise, each student assumes the role of an advocate for one side of a Yes/No debate on a preselected issue and must use their critical thinking skills to evaluate the strength and relevance of various arguments and reach a just decision on the issue. The exercise creates a chance for students to practice Ganong's decision-making types that establish a continuum from routine/rational to creative and assure the type that is carefully reflective and informed. Through matching debaters and setting objective success criteria based on completeness and relevance of argument, the teacher can help make sure the exercise challenges each student according to his ability, protects the self-confident nature of the thinker, and keeps practice within the zone of viable transfer for decision making and judgment.

Sharon A. Bailin, a philosopher and educational theorist, attempts to describe critical thinking in a way that suggests the need for the teacher to foster an excellent environment. In her book Achieving Extraordinary Ends: An Essay on Creativity, "What is crucial is a carefully conducted reflective judgment about what to believe or what to do. It sometimes involves thinking things through and in other cases it can involve careful delineation of the options," a statement that highlights the necessity of a classroom environment that challenges the student, promotes higher order thinking, and fosters reflective decision-making habits. This environment, according to Jane Roland Martin, must involve an open-ended structure where the teacher "sees the student as an active participant, a decision maker, a problem solver." Methods suggested to achieve this kind of classroom range from creating non-competitive environments, encouraging dialogue and debate, and bolstering confidence as an independent thinker through initiation of student-centered learning. All of which highlights the trust argued as necessary by Dewey and Martin in the critical thinker and the quality of his reflection and judgment.

CHAPTER 15

Promoting Collaboration

The theme of the story in this section is educational leadership. The principal, Marjorie Dudley, has the reputation of being a transformational leader, with the highest ethical qualities. This story is an illustration of her leadership in solving a problem in her school by approaching the problem in a different way. It is an example of how one person made a huge difference with his or her leadership. Dudley's role is a good example of how one person can be the change agent. "Morale as perceived by teachers is a robust predictor of achievement gains for the student body." If a principal's leadership can boost teacher morale, resulting in increased student achievement, this is a story worth studying. Dudley's leadership in this conflict would fit well into Marshall, Pattinson, and Maitland's four frames of leadership. This story places emphasis on the leadership qualities of one person, but also it aims to improve the school as a whole. So it will examine the decision-making context process, political, and resource frame of leadership.

CHAPTER 16

Adapting to Individual Needs

From this point forth, each chapter explores educators who embody a set of teaching principles that often lie outside the routines of traditional subject content. The first of these principles is that good teachers attend to the basic psychological needs of their students. We address this topic in Chapter 15, Humane Authority: Transforming a Bureaucratic Experience, introducing Victor Charlo, a high school dropout and pipefitter who became an extraordinary teacher of literature. "My teacher believed I was a genius," Charlo recalled, then corrected himself: "He made believe I was a genius, which was close enough." In the same way, reforming reading programs in elementary schools have high success rates when teachers act like they believe that all kids can learn. Teachers who change lives assume a primary responsibility for the students' academic and personal success. The stories we tell to illustrate this principle are legion, and most of the teachers in them show remarkable dedication to helping students help themselves. All involve clear, sometimes heroic enactments of the causes of self-regulated behavior and the learning strategies in which teachers play a part in schools that are knowledge producing. These will be the topics for the next four chapters.

CHAPTER 17

Building Resilience

Finally, a classroom called The Well has been developed for students with low attendance, behavior problems, or are at risk of disengagement. It teaches simple strategies for students to manage their emotions and be successful in school. These activities are monitored and supported through the Student Welfare Coordinator, Leading Teacher, and the School Focused Youth Service worker.

Other practical tasks, such as developing a homework policy, help students become more independent with their learning, improve organization, and develop a better home-school link. Regular physical activity and skills such as goal setting and task planning also help develop resilience by keeping students healthy and teaching persistence with goals.

Building resilience is something that ideally should be instilled in all young people in our schools. Resilience can be learned and developed, and the sooner it starts, the better. There are a range of activities that can foster resilience. These include establishing clubs such as the Lake Garden Club, Peer Mediation, and the Breakfast Club. These activities allow students to develop social skills, learn how to problem solve, and develop a sense of belonging in the school environment. This ultimately acts as a protective factor for students later on.

CHAPTER 18

Encouraging Self-Reflection

Almost by chance, I learned that encouraging students to reflect on their learning by asking thoughtful questions was the most important strategy in developing self-awareness, a skill that proved far more valuable than simply knowing the content. I usually asked these reflective questions on an exit (or end slip) after class, with the hopeful expectation that the student would ponder the question as opposed to writing the first thing that came to mind and then immediately forgetting about it. Specific reflective questions were most often asked when grading assessments or giving feedback, which produced more meaningful responses from students. I found that students were more receptive to these questions after not performing well on an assessment, as they were in a state of disequilibrium and were more likely to critically think about the cause of their confusion. Although I was not always questioning students directly, I learned to greatly increase wait-time after posing questions, giving students a quiet space to think. Often I would see students on the verge of an idea, but they would abort the process and change their answer if I did not respond within 1-2 seconds. Patience was key in waiting out these cognitive processes to show students that it is okay to struggle for a bit when thinking on a tough question. I also gave out journals to every student at the beginning of the year and would occasionally pose questions for them to ponder in their free time. I found these journals to be an excellent tool in tracking student thought and providing insight for future instruction.

CHAPTER 19

Fostering a Growth Mindset

Fostering a growth mindset within a student takes time and patience from the teacher. Frank believes that before educators can foster a growth mindset in students, they need to work on cultivating their own growth mindset and belief system about their students. Teachers must reflect on their own beliefs about their students' potential and ability. Frank suggests that there are teachers who believe students learn as a result of their teaching and those who learn as a result of their ability and potential. He adds, "Some teachers believe their role in the classroom is to bring out the potential in students, while others see it as their job to simply transmit information." Teachers with the former belief system are more likely to have a growth mindset about their students and be more successful in fostering a growth mindset in their students.

Children who believe that talents and abilities are things that can be developed over time with effort are more likely to succeed than children with a fixed mindset. A study led by Stanford University researcher Carol Dweck showed that children with the former mindset performed better in school than those with the latter mindset. Fostering a growth mindset in students is a difficult task to achieve for teachers, especially if students come with various dispositional beliefs about their intelligence. However, there are certain techniques and tactics that teachers can utilize to promote a growth mindset within their students as they take on tougher academic challenges.

CHAPTER 20

Teaching Beyond the Classroom

When we decided to write this book, we both felt that one of the most important aspects of our work was to inspire the next generation of teachers to choose this incredibly important profession. Because of this, a question that we asked in every interview was "What would you like to say to the next generation of teachers?" We wanted to end our interviews on this question, and we did not want to direct responses in any way. The responses were incredibly moving, and a common theme emerged. We thought that this was so important, that we dedicated an entire chapter of the book to these responses. The theme was that an inspirational teacher can have an incredibly far-reaching influence on the lives of students. This influence can genuinely affect the world in a very positive way. All of the teachers in our book acknowledged a mentor that they had in their early years of schooling, and credited those teachers with fostering their love of learning or their desire to enter the teaching profession. Those teachers changed the lives of the ones that followed, and the cycle continues. Any person with an inspirational teacher can give testimony to this. We decided that the final chapter of our book would serve to inspire as it had been inspired. We took the responses to the question of what advice each interviewee would give to the next generation of teachers, and grouped them in like categories. We then wrote an article that followed each category. This final chapter is a call to the next generation of teachers to "be the one". An article written by Alan Schoenfeld (chapter 21) probably best exemplifies the messages from these articles. We both feel that this is a very important piece of our work.

CHAPTER 21

Emphasizing Character Development

Was it not a lesson on character, for instance, that Ernie Williams learned from Doc Battin when as a student athletic trainer he was invited to spend Christmas vacation with the Battin family? "He didn't say anything," Ern recalls, "but the way they treated me in that beautiful home of theirs. I always had felt a grade above black people and here it was like we were all the same. That was the first time I experienced that kind of thing and it really opened my eyes." From Doc Dreisbach's independent work contract to Bazyl Pankulyn's tales of the old country, teachers provided Williams experiences and models to think about the kind of man he wanted to be. High on that list was the sort of rugged, independent woodsman epitomized by Reggie Coates and Ernie has spent a lifetime in the outdoors trying to build a camp like that of Reggie's in the Adirondacks. Finally, character is often best demonstrated in adversity and Ern provides no shortage of stories chronicling the influence of his teachers in the tough times of his life. He clearly recognizes in many cases the gifts and people he could have turned to for easier paths but has no regret at the choices the hard road has brought. Character is also the area in which Ernie feels he best carried on the legacy of his teachers, as a revered coach and teacher himself in the community of Lake Placid.

While much of today's educational discussion focuses on test scores, there are those who believe that the most important work of teachers occurs in character development. Character results from daily choices and is revealed when acted on; it is a complex behavior that must be taught through consistent example, discussion, and reflection. Who we are is the key determinant of how we will interpret and interact with the world around us. Good teachers understand this and over the years challenge students to think about and refine the nature of their character, for there is no sure way to prepare a child for the future than to equip him to choose well. Sometimes doing so saves a life. So important is this work that 12 of 34 teachers described character development as the primary task of teaching.

CHAPTER 22

Encouraging Curiosity

Griffith was a man with a profound love for learning and a peculiar and endearing man. He was fond of saying that the reason students couldn't learn from lectures in the past was because they didn't sit down and think about what their teacher was saying. He was very happy knowing that his students respected him and did learn, even though they couldn't learn all that he was trying to teach them. He loved chess and Huck Finn, blues and folk music, good food, and a 6-room white-columned cottage called Dogwood Place. He liked to travel and talk about various subjects with anyone who was also interested in learning the truth of things. He just wanted to know why things were the way they are.

Griffith first taught a very abstract theory of science and later developed a course comparing Greco-European and Pseudo-science medical systems. He also taught history of Western civilizations and a math course in the history and theory of probability.

Griffith was a man of great curiosity who sought to instill the same trait in his students. He was one of the most gifted teachers David Bond, an English professor at the University of New Orleans, ever had. Mr. Griffith taught history and theory of science, although he was not a scientist, in the tradition of the greatest cultural historians. He propounded that knowledge of the history and philosophy of science was essential for an understanding of society today. To him, science and technology are the most important and influential forces in today's world. Science cultures are analyzed in the same way as cultural historians and anthropologists analyze the cultures of various peoples. Griffith often said, "Science is culture." He taught that great theories are intimately connected to the unique historical context in which they were invented.

Encouraging Curiosity. Mr. Griffith (Bond) p. 225

CHAPTER 23

Supporting Student Goals

Jonathan Harrison recalls that some teachers who had a positive impact on him directly constructed pathways to success for students with performance or attendance problems. "I had a teacher that went out of her way to create more challenging work for me and find ways to get me involved in classroom activities. I remember her once calling my house and asking my parents to put me at the head of the table while we were having dinner. This effort reaped great results in my English grades and always stuck with me as an example of a teacher genuinely caring about a student's success." A study by the National Center for Educational Statistics found that students who feel that their teachers truly care about them are more likely to take an active and leading role in their own learning to achieve their personal targets.

Paul Riggieri remembers a teacher who genuinely cared about him. "He was so interested in me and it really motivated me to care." Teachers have a tremendous opportunity to nurture a student's academic and social confidence. They can encourage them to pursue and reach their goals, create leadership opportunities, provide resources and moral support at crucial times, and set up positive peer and mentor relationships.

CHAPTER 24

Igniting Passion for a Subject

Miss Miralda Clifton, Head of the Senior History Department at Methodist Ladies' College, Melbourne, has a specific goal: to nourish within her students a 'love affair with history'. The steps she takes towards realization of that ambition are many. As well as efficient organization of each course she teaches, Miss Clifton displays an infectious enthusiasm which arises from her own continuing interest in and research on historical events. At every point during her exposition of some fact or event to her students, she interjects a related story or anecdote, frequently with some contemporary parallel, by way of illustration. Her intention here is to 'spread out' the event and make it 'come alive', and it is frequently the humorous or tragic narrative which Miss Clifton's students will remember, rather than the hard fact itself. It is significant that each year, when asked for their comments on a departing class, Miss Clifton's colleagues should spontaneously use the following phrase in one form or another: 'Well, that was obviously a history class!'

The typical stereotype of the eccentric science teacher whose passion is catching also describes teachers of languages or history who manage to pass their subject through the gift of interesting classroom storytelling. Yet the author has interviewed somebody from each subject area and is convinced that the common ground these teachers share is a solid background knowledge of their subject, coupled with an enthusiasm which ignites like tinder when communicated to the students.

CHAPTER 25

Creating a Sense of Belonging

Our knowledge of belonging has been modified throughout Heath Administration. Boomerang, the first text under study, emphasizes a sense of belonging to family, tribe, and native land, as well as the Aboriginal ways, a connection that no longer exists for the Australian people. Culture and origins greatly influence our identity, and this painting conveys that it is a source of contentment and security. Boomerang itself symbolizes return, and it's the return to one's roots that today, many Australians are in search of. This painting has given our group a first and deeper understanding of belonging and its links to identity.

Belonging is a fundamental human emotion. People need to feel a sense of belonging and acceptance among their social groups, regardless of whether these groups are large organizations or small cliques. While some people experience a strong sense of belonging, others may feel estranged and rejected. It is essential to build a sense of belonging as it can affect an individual's perception of their own identity. This concept of belonging can be explored through a variety of texts. These texts may include the poetry of Peter Skrzynecki and Immigrant Chronicle, the song "Father and Son" by Cat Stevens, and the novel The Red Tree by Shaun Tan. Each of these texts has strong connections to the statement and effectively displays a positive or negative sense of belonging.

CHAPTER 26

Teaching Empathy and Compassion

In an extra ticket booth of a farmhouse hermitage of a school, kindness became art, and the headmaster took the time and effort to teach all of us to be kind and thoughtful by his great example and providing a basis for our own lives of serious, serviceable empathy and compassion. He despised the Greek military junta, and he took the almost unprecedented step of marching the student body out to the middle of the hard Texas winter and trying to make us feel, by demanding of us how we could feel no distress for suffering people, the cold and the worry of the Greeks. We learned to question our concern for less fortunate others by reading Animal Farm. We always projected our roles in responding to the plight of the homeless, the disabled, the ward of the state, or the old person dispossessed or abandoned. It is only now that I have learned the difficulty of taking special needs children on field trips. We can hope the children of these adult lives are as empathetic as the scared college freshman he took, who went on to realize that empathy and compassion must thrive in the wider community and internationally through social, public and economic policy, and to argue and face on the good fight. This headmaster had no time for the social and economic status-based biases he saw in other schools. I became a teacher. This is his lesson, put into practice of my own high school community, that may mean the most to me, and that I may have now begun to realize as much as time and place suffer in context. This man is one of my life heroes, and I have told him so. Teachers who change lives.

CHAPTER 27

Promoting Global Awareness

Promoting global awareness involves helping students to see their lives in a larger context, encouraging them to become citizens of the world. Teachers do this by giving students a point of comparison for appreciating their own customs and traditions, while using this self-awareness as a takeoff point for understanding other cultural perspectives. This process includes helping students to understand the interconnectedness of world societies, identifying both global challenges and successes. A teacher who promoted global awareness recalls starting a current events discussion with her third graders following the Gulf War. "That day I cringed at the thought of explaining to young children why and how we had war," she says, "But very quickly I was surprised and impressed at how much they knew. In fact, they taught me a few things. I realized then that they are capable of grasping so much more than we often give them credit for." By maintaining high expectations, this teacher and others like her hope to develop an informed generation of future decision-makers. Students who understand the ramifications of today's actions well beyond their own borders can become responsible global citizens.

CHAPTER 28

Building Positive Relationships

Positive relationships with students are the backbone of every great teacher. This chapter outlines how legendary teacher Eugene Eubanks, lovingly known as "Captain," fostered and developed enduring, meaningful relationships with his students. Captain astutely realized the value of building positive relationships early in his career. He was fond of repeating a saying he'd heard, "No one cares how much you know, until they know how much you care." Captain states he made the best gains with his students when he "got the conversation to anything other than school." The fact he knew students well led to their greater respect for him. His stronger rapport with his students led to more open lines of communication and thus, better teaching. According to Captain, one of the most effective ways for teachers to get to know their students is to observe them carefully, both in the class and at play. In doing so, teachers will find out the student's strengths and weaknesses, likes and dislikes. This knowledge is invaluable. "It's power in that, in trying to teach that child," he says. "When a teacher realizes a kid can do something, he's more inclined to get the child to do it." By targeting students' specific talents, interests, and areas needing improvement, teachers can develop lesson plans and projects tailor-suited to individual students. The results will be increased student confidence and self-esteem. Eubanks also asserts that his caring knowledge of kids gave him "the right to correct 'em and the right to praise 'em." This right is clearly affirmed when it comes from a teacher who knows the student well and has the student's best interests at heart. Students are eager to please and more willing to accept criticism from a teacher they know truly cares for them. Eubanks employed these principles in his classes at every grade level and the success he experienced, both as a teacher and a mentor to students, is testimony to the effectiveness of his methods. His approach to fostering positive relationships between teacher and student can easily be adapted to any educational setting and promises great rewards.

CHAPTER 29

Celebrating Achievements

We continue to celebrate the fantastic work of teachers in Buckinghamshire with a special award ceremony on 15th May. The ceremony, held at The Elgiva Theatre in Chesham, recognized the successes of teachers who have completed their induction year and newly qualified teachers (NQTs) who have successfully completed the induction process. This year, over 150 teachers from across the county gained recognition for successful completion of induction/NQT year. Dignitaries included local MPs, LEA officers, Governors and Headteachers alongside the friends and families of those receiving awards. This event has clearly demonstrated that our teachers represent their profession in a highly commendable way and everyone attending the event would agree that it is important to celebrate the successes of our colleagues. A full list of all those who gained induction success can be found on NUT website. What constitutes a successful induction year or NQT? Whilst this may vary between individuals and there is no precise definition of what success actually looks like, we felt that it would be beneficial to speak to teachers who have satisfied the criteria and find out what they believe has contributed to their success. By determining what has proved successful for others we may be able to offer some positive guidance to teachers still partway through or about to embark upon their induction year/NQT. Throughout this term we intend to publish a series of short articles written by successful NQTs on the NUT website which will give some insight to the experiences of those who have recently transitioned from ITT to qualified teacher.

CHAPTER 30

Leaving a Lasting Impact

For example, one student from Algoma, Wisconsin, was inspired by his history teacher to become an educator. Many years later, that student became a language arts teacher and began to correspond with his former history instructor and mentor. This correspondence resulted in a collection of nearly 100 letters and artifacts that illuminated the teacher's 35-year career and led to the writing of a book about the teacher. This former student continues to share the stories and lessons of his former history teacher with his college students.

A teacher's work is never done. Even once they retire or pass away, an extraordinary teacher can make an impact. In this section, many stories featured contain students who were inspired to do something for the teacher that once inspired them. This teacher's influence may come in the form of a student choosing to go into teaching or a student making the choice to succeed in something that a teacher didn't think possible. Many people go back to their favorite teachers years or decades after they were taught, wanting to say thank you for what was done for them.

CHAPTER 31

Conclusion

The book is also a useful tool for personal reflection and professional development. We all know that teachers have a lasting impact on their students, yet it is so easy to become immersed in the day-to-day challenges of teaching and to lose sight of the greater purpose. Reading these stories reminds us of the power of positive relationships and the potential to influence the lives of students in a positive way. We have found the stories of persistence and tenacity in the face of difficult students and difficult circumstances to be particularly grounding. At certain times in our careers, we may find such persistence to be a challenge.

Sharing the stories of truly great teachers who have committed their professional lives to the development of children has generated a range of emotions. Each story is different, yet there are strong common strands. These teachers are inspirational. They teach us that all kids are important, that education does make a difference to people's lives, and that teaching really can be a lifelong and fulfilling career. These stories have left us with a strong affirmation of our choice of career and a deeper understanding of the work we do. Future generations of teachers need well-researched and well-written material such as this to inspire them and to pass the message that teaching is an important and worthwhile vocation.

A large part of the motivation for compiling such a book as "Teachers Who Changed Our Lives" was to create a lasting legacy for the profession. Despite significant strides in the 90s, the teaching profession has sometimes been on the nose with the community at large. Teachers and education in general have been a popular whipping boy for politicians and the media, and teachers report a loss of community respect as a result. The older generation of teachers and the good old days are romanticized, and yet the stories we hear from older teachers are not so different from those of today. They faced the same challenges, and they would argue that, in fact, schools are a much better place for kids than they ever were.